MEMORY LANE
ROCHDALE

ROCHDALE
METROPOLITAN BOROUGH
COUNCIL

MEMORY LANE
ROCHDALE

Rochdale
Observer

JOHN COLE AND RICHARD CATLOW

breedon **books**
PUBLISHING

First published in Great Britain in 2001 by
The Breedon Books Publishing Company Limited
Breedon House, 3 The Parker Centre, Derby, DE21 4SZ.

ISBN 1 85983 273 3

Printed and bound by Butler & Tanner, Frome,
Somerset, England.

Jacket printing by GreenShires, Leicester, England.

Contents

Introduction

WHEN local historian John Cole and *Observer* editor-in-chief Richard Catlow were researching their hugely popular book *Images of Rochdale*, they unearthed so many superb photographs it soon became clear that one book alone could never come close to doing justice to this rich collection. So the natural answer was to produce a second book and here is that follow-up *Memory Lane Rochdale*.

Like *Images*, this new book draws on a formula that is quite different from most books of old photographs.

The past began yesterday and although you'll find no pictures here that are quite so modern, this collection runs from the early days of photography to include the 1950s, 1960s and 1970s, and even a few from the 1980s.

People particularly enjoy the history that they lived through themselves and sometimes we forget just how much the town has changed over the last few decades.

Have you forgotten how friendly and welcoming the old Rochdale market was? Can you remember the buildings that stood where those of the 1970s now dominate? Do you recall the shops and offices you used to visit on Yorkshire Street? Allow us to indulge you in a bit of nostalgia because it will all come back to you here.

At the same time, the past we don't remember can be equally fascinating. In these pages you'll find what is almost certainly the oldest surviving photograph of Rochdale, taken an unbelievable century and a half ago.

There's a specially-researched section on the firm which could claim, with some justification, to have built Rochdale. You'll be amazed at how many well-known buildings they were responsible for.

Every community within the *Observer's* circulation area is catered for, from Whitworth through to Castleton and Littleborough and Milnrow. You'll find idyllic rural scenes, and industrial scenes so grim that even L. S. Lowry would have blenched.

There are pageants and parades, triumphs and tragedies. Indeed, the whole of Rochdale life is here.

When that first book was published in 1996, it soon sold out and was reprinted. At the time, the remark was made that it was the result of the *Rochdale Observer*, Rochdale Metropolitan Borough Council, and the people of Rochdale, all coming together to produce something that was worthy of the town. The same can be said again and as we begin our journey into the 21st century, there can be no harm at all in looking back over the 20th century, and into the 19th, to remind ourselves of Rochdale's heritage.

Rochdale Remembered

A drawing of South Parade in 1780 with Butts House on the centre left and the former Wellington Hotel at the bottom of Drake Street on the right.

A view of Rochdale from Broadfield. On the right is the grammar school at Sparrow Hill which was built in 1847 and demolished in 1904, to be replaced by the nurses' home now the Broadfield Hotel.

A drawing of Rochdale centre in the mid-19th century showing the bottom of Yorkshire Street on the right and old stone bridge leading to South Parade. St Chad's Church can just be seen in the left background. Today the scene would be dominated by the Town Hall on the left bank of the river.

Probably the earliest known photograph of Rochdale, the scene shows Manchester Road in the late 1860s.

The same area in the 1960s.

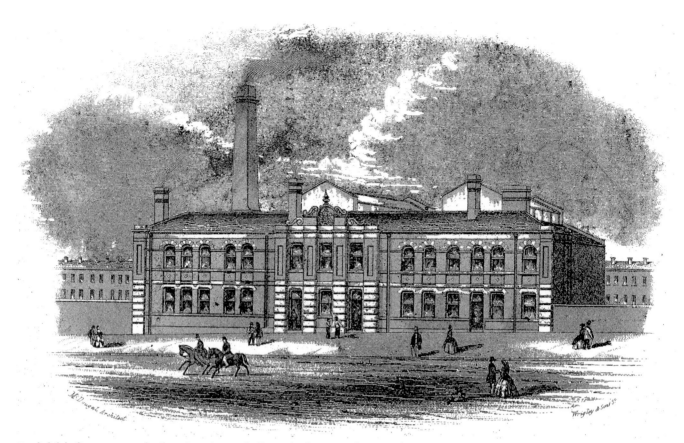

Rochdale's first purpose-built swimming and slipper baths opened at Smith Street in 1868 at Lea Hall, renamed the Broadwater Centre. The Baths Inn still recalls the building's original function.

A rare shot of the Town Hall under construction in 1868 with, we think, the architect William Crosland in the foreground witnessing the raising of one of the great roof trusses.

A view across the Entwisle Road area around 1870. This was a vista L.S. Lowry would have loved.

The old Central Library opened in 1885, prior to the addition of the art gallery. The building was being upgraded at the time of writing to house the borough's new Arts and Heritage Centre, restoring Rochdale's museum to its original site.

Packer Street around 1890, looking up to
the parish church with Leyland Chambers
in the centre.

The opening of the Reform Club on Drake Street in April 1896. Taking its name from the Rochdale Reform Association and the Reform Acts which created modern democracy, this was in fact the club for the local Liberal Party and was opened by Lord Roseberry, the Liberal Party leader. A rare election defeat in Rochdale, the party's first in more than 30 years, led members to decide that this central premises – it stood on the corner of Drake Street and Water Street – was needed. The building, previously a hotel, was leased to them at a peppercorn rent by Sir James Duckworth. Later the club moved to Holly Bank, also on Drake Street. The club finally closed in 1966.

Looking along South Parade. The Robin Hood Hotel is on the left of the picture.

The centre of Rochdale dominated by the Kelsall and Kemp's mills on the site of the modern 'Black Box' and bus station.

Amen Corner in 1908. This was the 'Great House' built by the Gartside family in the late 16th century which ended its days as a lodging house for homeless men.

The 'new' billiards hall at Nelson Street in 1909. The building is better known nowadays as the Chicago Rock Night Club.

A busy scene in Manchester Road, Castleton, around 1910.

The Junior Boys' playroom at Buckley Hall in the early 1900s. The building was established as an orphanage in 1888 by the Christian Brothers of Charity and operated until just before its diamond jubilee in 1947. Former pupils attended reunions until the 1980s.

A surprisingly rural scene in built-up Balderstone as cows and workers make their way home. St Mary's Church is in the background.

The Church Steps and Packer Street. The photographer has caused a lot of interest.

Looking across the old Firgrove Bridge (before it was widened) in about 1902. The Lord Nelson Hotel is centre picture with Belfield Lane running off to the left.

A very early photograph looking along St Mary's Gate. The little girls on the steps at the right look to be in their Sunday best.

Enjoying a stroll up Shawclough Road. A splendid example of that Rochdale speciality, the stone-flag wall, can be seen on the right.

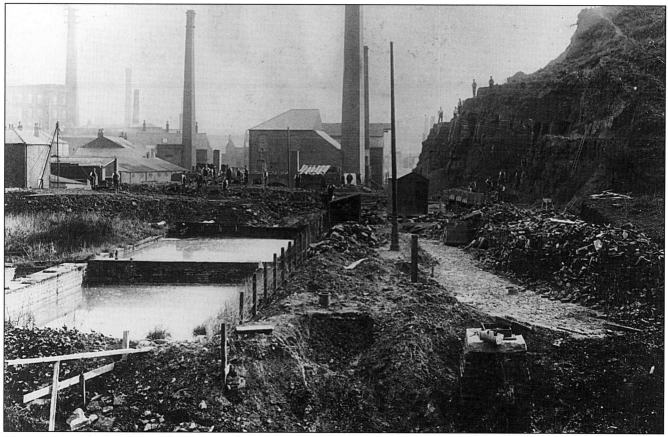

The creation of Mellor Street. The rocks on the right can still be seen today.

This beats a pram! A donkey-drawn child's carriage pictured at Edenfield Road, Passmonds in 1900.

Ellen Wallace, a local wisewoman better known as Nell Racker pictured with her grandson outside Belfield Cottage around 1910. The current *Rochdale Observer* has a weekly column written by a male member of staff which was christened Neil Racker in her honour.

The splendid John Bright Room in the old Central Library contained Bright's personal memorabilia and the bookcase, purchased by public subscription to celebrate the repeal of the Corn Laws.

Early cars outside the Flying Horse Hotel shortly after it was rebuilt.

A proud gardener. Mr Arthur Walpole of Jutland Avenue Gardens in 1922.

Dunkirk and Dunkirk House in 1932. This stood on the site of Dunkirk Rise and the College Bank flats. And (below) after demolition.

Looking along the newly-built Queensway in 1925 with Arrow Mill in the background.

The Castleton end of Queensway, off Manchester Road.

Looking up Rooley
Moor Road from
Spotland Bridge.

An aerial view of the Syke housing estate in August 1938. Syke Common is beyond with Buckley Hall towards the distant right.

Town Meadows looking south in 1949 when work was under way on creating the sunken gardens.

Rochdale centre gets the floodlight treatment in the 1930s.

A reminder of the bad side of days-gone-by in this picture of Barrack Yard.

This cannon was an attraction in Broadfield Park until World War Two when it was probably melted down, along with countless railings, for the war effort.

The old library and art gallery in the 1930s.

A bustling scene on Broadway. I'll bet that dustbin was awkward to carry home!

Broadway, dominated by Burtons the Tailors, in 1958. The present Barclays Bank was then a branch of Martins, a Liverpool firm that was later taken over by its bigger rival.

Broadway at just after
midday on a summer's
day in 1958.

Smith Street with Electric House on the left.

Sunset over Albert Royds Street.

Newgate in the 1950s.

A627
NEWGATE

A bustling scene in Drake Street in 1955. Someone had a very smart car. We think it is an Alvis.

This old aerial photograph shows Woodbine Street and the Oldham Road area with the Rochdale Canal running to the top right of the picture. On the bottom left is the original Wellfield Surgery with its large garden at the rear.

The Swan with Two Necks on Oldham Road in the early 1950s. The taxi service from the Rialto Garage was 'open till midnight'.

A wintry view in 1959, looking east from Oldham Road along the Rochdale Canal.

An early 1960s scene at the junction of Oldham and Milnrow Roads at Wet Rake Gardens. The building with the clock once housed the Operative Cotton Spinners' Association with Fletcher Bolton's timber merchants next door but one.

An aerial view of the town centre in 1966 showing the recently-completed flats at College Bank, the cricket field (with play under way). Falinge Park is at the top of the picture and Broadfield Park bottom right. It looks as though work is still to be completed on St Mary's Way as a section of the road is still cordoned off and the tiny figures of what must be road contractors can just be made out.

The new police station under construction. Beyond it homes and the cricket ground occupied the land now home to Asda and Curry's.

A study in 1960s cars on Yorkshire Street in 1966. The Curry's shop, left, was rather smaller than its modern successor.

Plenty of shoppers in Yorkshire Street in the days prior to redevelopment.

The old Yorkshire Street starts to disappear in this picture of the early 1970s when work began on the market redevelopment.

Looking up Toad Lane in 1970.

St Mary's Gate with
the College Bank
flats under
construction.

The town centre in the early 1970s, with the Salvation Army HQ in the background and the Hippodrome Theatre on the left.

Looking across the Packer Spout area in 1971. Note how much the trees and bushes in the park have grown since then. The modern building (centre right), now gone, was council offices. Behind it spot the Mecca Bingo sign.

Looking more like *Coronation Street's* 'Weatherfield' than Rochdale, this dense sea of housing, looking across from the Entwistle Road railway viaduct in the early 1970s, shows Ramsey Street, with College Bank flats and St John's Church, Wardleworth in the background.

Taken from Mardyke, one of the College Bank flats in the late 1960s, this picture shows Toad Lane the market and the town centre beyond.

The Municipal Offices
from River Street in
1975 contrast starkly
with the old mill in
the foreground.

A view from the
College Bank flats
looking east over
Mitchell Street in
1975.

The town centre in 1970. Note the impressive light that stood in the road and Williams Deacons Bank.

A contrast in towers, between the old Salvation Army and the then-new shopping centre in 1979.

A view over Rochdale to Blackstone Edge from Marland Golf Course in 1980.

Rochdale town centre in 1980 when the Regal Cinema was undergoing one of its changes in ownership, this time by EMI.

A pleasant scene along the Esplanade in 1978.

Workmen on Toad Lane in 1980 creating the conservation area around Rochdale and the world's first co-operative store.

A view across the old library to College Bank flats in 1980. The library is now being transformed into Rochdale's Arts and Heritage Centre.

The town centre in 1983.

A scene from 1981 as youngsters play among rubbish overlooked by the now-demolished Ashfield Valley flats.

The original St Aidan's Church at Marland Old Road which was built by famous Middleton architect Edgar Wood in an Art Deco style that was very much the cutting edge of international taste. It was replaced by a much more old-fashioned looking building designed by a Mr Temple Moore, described as being the 'High Priest of Gothic'.

The Strand at Kirkholt in 1984.

That Was The Day...!

When Rochdale businessman Clement Royds became High Sheriff of Lancashire in 1850 it was seen as a sign that Rochdale had really 'arrived'. Consequently a triumphal arch was built and even the fire brigade tender was brought into use in the parade that saw him leaving for Liverpool.

Battle of Waterloo veterans in the Vicarage Gardens in 1856 before taking the train to Manchester to witness the inauguration of a 32ft high bronze statue of the Duke of Wellington outside the Manchester Infirmary. Note the medals pinned proudly to their chests. It's an amazing thing to look into these faces and to think that were in action back in 1815.

Littleborough Square is heaving for the celebration of Queen Victoria's Diamond Jubilee in 1897.

These fountains on the Holme were brought in specially to help celebrate Victoria's Diamond Jubilee in 1897. How about some today to add character to the Butts?

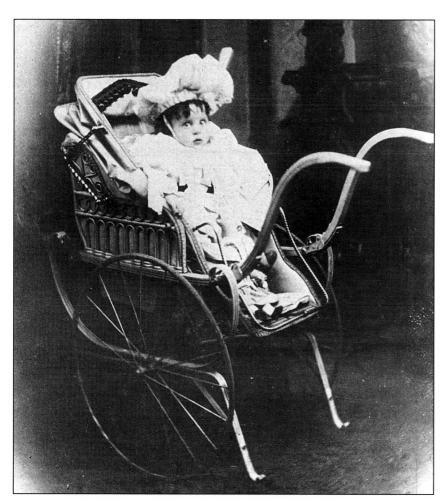

To mark Queen Victoria's Diamond Jubilee in 1897, local firm Orrells of Drake Street gave a pram to the first baby born.

There was a fantastic turnout in the Town Hall Square in 1904 to mark the centenary of the birth of Rochdale MP and statesman Richard Cobden. Along with that other local hero John Bright he had won the repeal of the Corn Laws, opening up the prospect of cheaper food for working people and a decisive move away from agricultural to industrial interests in the running of Britain.

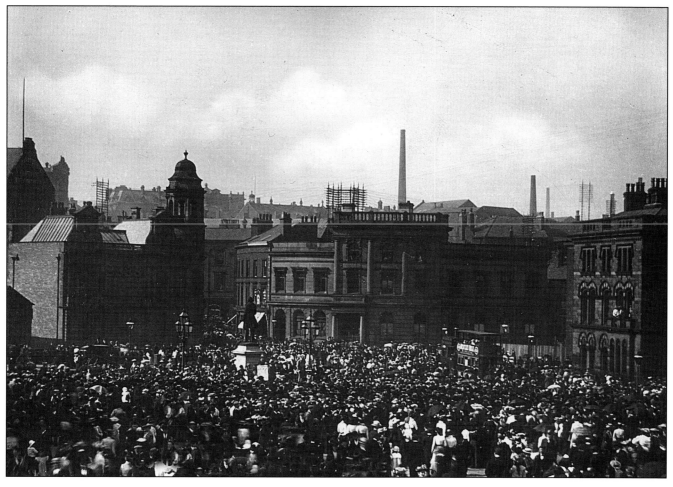

In 1902, when he was Mayor, Coun (later Alderman) Samuel Turner announced that he would give Mount Falinge House and its grounds to the town to become a park and would also give an extra £2,500 to go towards planting. Alderman Turner, whose money came from the family business of Turner Brothers, the asbestos manufacturers, was asked to perform the opening ceremony once the Prince of Wales had declined the invitation. This was in August 1905. The house, only the façade of which now remains, was previously home to the Royds family. It was already in poor condition at the time.

The Municipal Jubilee procession passes the Town Hall in 1906.

Drake Street and the *Observer* Buildings on the left were decorated in this picture taken for the Municipal Jubilee in 1906.

Drake Street in 1906
with the bunting up
for the Rochdale
Jubilee celebrations.

Crowds watch a procession along Yorkshire Street to Hamer Corner for the 1906 Municipal Jubilee.

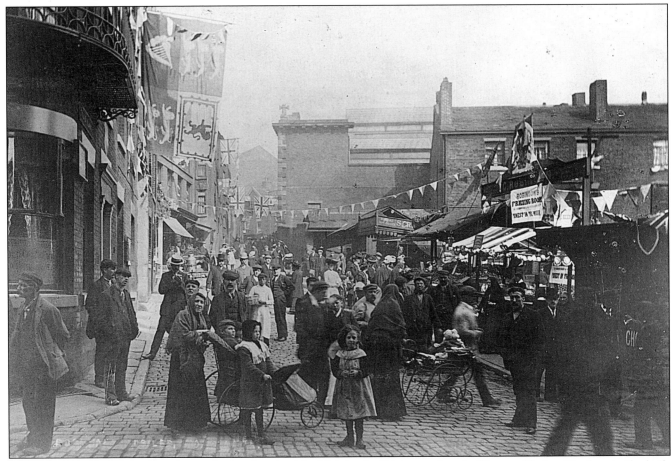

This marvellous picture of Toad Lane during the Municipal Jubilee in 1906 was taken by Thomas Pinder. The boy in the bath chair is Arnold Eaton. He worked in a slaughter house, fell in a vat and had to have a leg amputated, but still lived to a ripe old age.

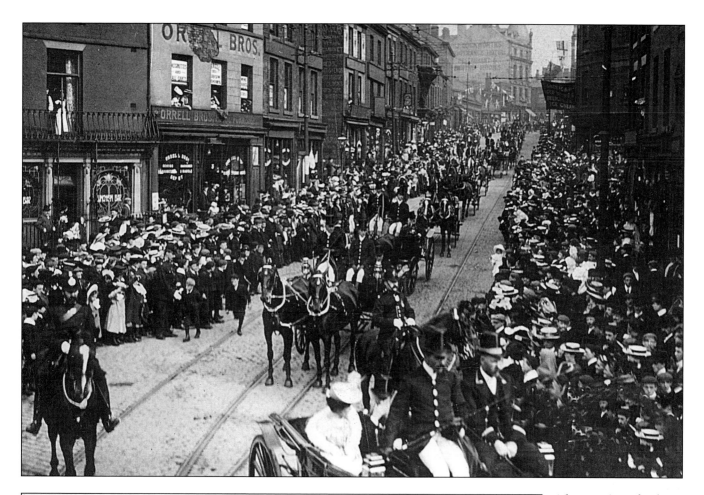

The opening of Falinge Park was a red-letter day for Rochdale. Here part of the procession which celebrated it is seen coming down Drake Street.

The celebrations for the coronation of George V in 1911 must have involved the whole town. Every vantage point was taken – even the roof of the Flying Horse, while the banking up to St Chad's was completely packed.

King George V and Queen Mary on the special town centre podium at the heart of their visit to Rochdale in 1913.

World War One is over and the Rochdale Peace Celebration passes the Castle Inn at Pinfold on Manchester Road. Drake Street runs to the right.

Gracie Fields, on one of her visits back to Rochdale, makes a pot of tea in the kitchen of her friend's home at 2 Milkstone Road. The date is 1933, when the singer/actress was already an international star.

Part of the celebrations for the silver jubilee of King George V in 1935 was this ox roasting on the Cattle Market.

The silver jubilee celebrations for King George V and Queen Mary in 1935 were amongst the most splendid in Rochdale's history. This is just part of the procession witnessed by the crowd looking across from the Town Hall.

On 21 January 1936, Edward VIII was proclaimed king from the balcony at Rochdale Town Hall. The monarch was never to be crowned and abdication came later.

Scenes from the royal visit to Rochdale in 1938 with the then new King and Queen (now the Queen Mother) drawing the crowds in the Town Hall Square.

A nation celebrates; in this case with a VE Day street party at Clover Hall Crescent, Belfield.

Labour cabinet minister Herbert Morrison on a visit to Rochdale. His wife was a local girl.

The visit of Queen Elizabeth (now the Queen Mother) to Rochdale in June 1948.

Castleton Moor Conservative Club was well decorated for the coronation festivities of 1953.

The roundabout in the town centre become an illuminated maypole for the town's centenary celebrations in 1956.

A parade of police vehicles passes the Post Office in 1957 to celebrate the force's centenary.

The Mayoral Procession in 1967. The Mayor was Henry Howarth. More easily recognised is Cyril Smith, on his right, who was deputy mayor.

The Rochdale Arts Festival of August 1971, pictured occupying the Town Hall car park, was a pioneering event for its time and was probably one of the first outdoor events to be built around the arts rather than royal celebrations or fairground-style entertainments. It was a forerunner of today's Streets Ahead festival.

Princess Anne chats to two local women in the Town Hall during her visit to Rochdale in March 1975.

Wardleworth in the early 1980s with locals in celebratory mood after the opening of the new extension to the local community centre.

Prince Charles visits the Kashmiri Youth Project (KYP) as part of the organisation's 10th birthday celebrations in September 1989.

These We Have Lost

This picture shows the strange war memorial which Richard (Dickie) Kenyon erected to honour the British victory at Bunker Hill in the American War of Independence (though the actual battle was fought at nearby Breeds Hill!) It bears no inscription and was once used as a 'rubbing stoop' for his cattle. Kenyon lived at Meadowcroft House (later Beaumonds) and farmed the land along the banks of the Roach at Lower Bamford. The district became known as 'Bunkers Hill'.

This impressive waterwheel was at Roads Mill, Wardle, now submerged beneath Watergrove Reservoir.

The Cottage Homes between Wardle and Shore were opened in 1900; though they look newer than that. They are believed to have been built under Poor Law Public Assistance legislation and cost £17,000. In each lived a house mother who had care of a group orphan children whose navy blue uniform made them familiar figures around the town. Later the homes were to provide holidays for underprivileged children from Manchester and Salford and for convalescent soldiers in World War One. After World War Two the homes became a borstal before closure and demolition.

The demolition of Castleton Hall in 1905 meant that the area lost one of its finest buildings. Built in the late 16th century, the building latterly became the headquarters of Thomas Champness Joyful News Mission, which subsequently transferred to the Champness Hall in Drake Street.

The Old Clock Face inn in Lord Street. The Exchange shopping centre stands here now. It was the site of the birthplace of the dialect writer Edwin Waugh.

John Bright's statue when it was in Town Hall Square before being relocated to Broadfield Park. Why not bring it back to where more people would see it?

JOHN BRICHT

BORN 16TH NOV. 1811
DIED 27TH MARCH 1889.

BE JUST AND FEAR NOT

Before the river was bridged over, this scene at Newgate shows a particularly old corner of Rochdale.

WINE LODGE

HONESTY EXCELLENCE AND PURITY

The Orchard (as it was then known) on the left and the Esplanade in 1909 before the river was covered over when the latter name was applied to the whole road.

Broadley wool and cotton mill in 1870 stood in the valley above Healey Dell. By the turn of the century it was ruined.

The dethronement of King Cotton gathers pace. The chimney of Derby Mill at Woodbine Street is felled in 1966.

The Three Cups coffee house at Sudden in 1906. This magnificent-looking building was demolished to make way for the Roch Valley Way.

There's nothing that new about daft and meaningless pub names. How many people remember the Burlington Bertie pub on Bury-Rochdale Old Road? This photograph of the pub, nowadays the much more traditional Dog and Partridge, was taken in 1983.

The old Rochdale Manor House (more commonly referred to as 'The Orchard') stood on the banks of the River Roch facing the Town Hall.

The Manor House was the family home of the Deardens who purchased the Manor from Lord Byron, the poet, in 1822. The poet's father is pictured here.

Mills, Muck and Brass

Henry Nuttall, of Castle Works, Rochdale, was the country's leading supplier of ranges to fish and chip shops. This splendid example, obviously ready for showing in a parade, could be heated by coal, gas or electricity.

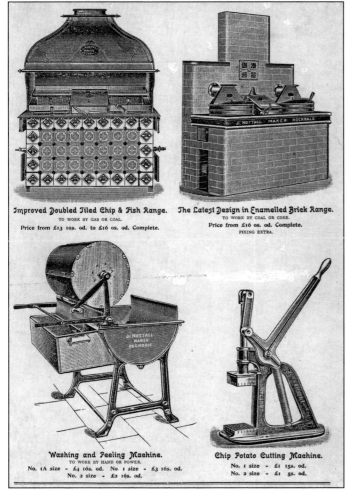

Improved Doubled Tiled Chip & Fish Range.
TO WORK BY GAS OR COAL.
Price from £13 10s. 0d. to £16 0s. 0d. Complete.

The Latest Design in Enamelled Brick Range.
TO WORK BY COAL OR COKE.
Price from £16 0s. 0d. Complete.
FIXING EXTRA.

Washing and Peeling Machine.
TO WORK BY HAND OR POWER.
No. 1A size - £4 16s. 0d.   No. 1 size - £3 16s. 0d.
No. 2 size - £2 16s. 0d.

Chip Potato Cutting Machine.
No. 1 size - £1 15s. 0d.
No. 2 size - £1 5s. 0d.

Nuttall's fish and chip ranges were world leaders. Here's a poster outlining some of the firm's products in the 1890s. The firm, based at Regent Mill, on Regent Street, began trading in 1861 in a small, back street shop run by a former blacksmith. The firm supplied its wares around the world and also had strong links with the defence industry. In World War One, Nuttall's horse-drawn ranges ploughed through the mud of Flanders. In more recent times the firm made galleys for nuclear submarines.

These hard-working fellows at Newhey are pictured with their crusher (or kibbling) machine. Stone not good enough for use in building was crushed to make a gravel for laying on roads.

This picture from 1979 shows Holcroft's castings and forgings works at Townhead.

Castleton Moor Mill pictured around 1910. The company was established on Nixon Street in 1900 and the building later became the town's first Asda store.

The warehouse of Robert Taylor Heape and Son in 1902. The street is Baillie Street. This photograph dates from just after Heape's death, when the considerable family fortune passed to Robert's son Benjamin.

An aerial photograph from the years just before the M62 was built shows the mills alongside Trows Lane at Castleton in a very rural setting.

Tub making was a skilled craft at the Rochdale Corporation Cleansing Department.

Mellor Street brickworks. A few remains still exist on the site.

Bank Mill was a classic early mill building.

Eclipse Mill on Buckley Road was built in 1899 and opened in 1900. It had more than 118,000 mule spindles in its heyday. The firm was founded by a group of local businessmen including Alderman Miles Ashworth, who as Mayor of Rochdale had the honour of cutting the first sod when work began on the site. The Ashworths were to remain closely associated with the mill. Later extensions and improvements meant the workforce went from 150 to more than 500 people and included a canteen capable of seating 240. Staff were treated to a day trip to Blackpool in July 1950, to celebrate the firm's golden jubilee. But, a few years later the clouds gathering over the Lancashire cotton industry meant Eclipse Mill announced its closure in 1959 The building was bought by mail order firm John Noble Ltd.

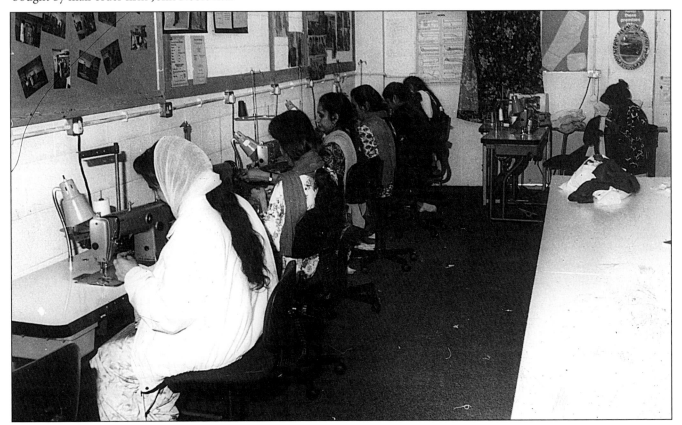

Sewing workshop at the Kashmir Youth Project in 1990.

Alderglen Mill and a fine old tree at Spotland Bridge in 1974. The factory achieved some notoriety by employing women from the Philippines who, at one stage, were said to have been locked in overnight to protect them from the dangers of Rochdale's night life.

Collingwood's peeler factory at March Street.

Pipes a plenty at Ashworth's clayworks at Littleborough. Ralph Ashworth's Starring coal and fire clay factory operated from the mid-19th century.

Work under way inside Ashworth's.

Inside Ashworth's clay works at Littleborough.

RALPH ASHWORTH & Co.,
LIMITED,
STARRING COAL AND FIRE CLAY WORKS,
LITTLEBOROUGH,
MANUFACTURERS OF
SANITARY TUBES,
FIRE BRICKS, BOILER BLOCKS,
Flue Tiles, Chimney Pots, Tops, &c.

Every description of Fireclay Goods,
Glazed and Unglazed, made to order.

MANCHESTER DEPOT:---50, GRANBY ROW,
OFF OLD GARRATT.

Advertisements for Ashworth's products from a directory of 1873.

This magnificent double beam engine was inside Town Head Mill, Rochdale. Constructed in 1863 at the Phoenix Foundry, Whitehall Street, it was dismantled in 1946 after 83 years continuous service.

This little coal mine was a feature of the Ashworth Valley in the 19th century. Now nature has reclaimed the site.

In June 1950 someone had the bright idea of capturing craftsmen at work in dying trades. At the time, blacksmith John William Meeks, of Ramsden Road, Wardle, was already 90 years old.

The pair of tandem compound engines at Clover Mill, Rochdale, pictured in 1953. Like so much of Rochdale's industrial heritage these magnificent machines are no more.

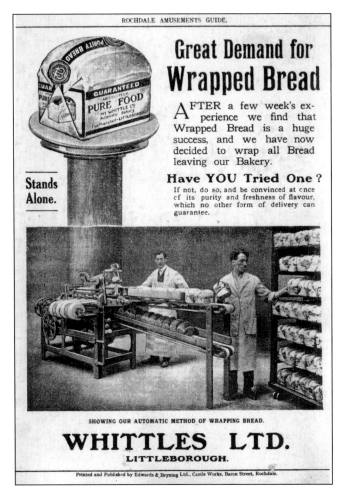

Motor mechanics training at the Kashmir Youth Project (KYP) in 1993.

A great idea from Whittles of Littleborough. Whittle's was founded in 1893 and became a limited company in 1911. The firm always prided itself on its innovation, introducing its regionally-distributed 'Purity 8' loaf in the 1930s.

I'll Buy That!

A familiar Rochdale sight in 1910 was this horse-drawn ice cream van.

The Maypole Dairy store at Yorkshire Street in 1910 with the smartly-dressed staff standing proudly outside.

Robert Hall's shop at the corner of Harehill Road, Littleborough has a fine display of enamelled signs on its walls. The picture was taken about 1910.

Bill Fox was a famous black pea vendor in Rochdale.

A laden cart pauses outside the Wardleworth Brow branch of the Pioneers with Wardleworth Station in the background. Among its goods is cube sugar from Henry Tate and Sons of London.

Sutcliffe and Ashworth's shop on Drake Street in the 1930s. Sutcliffe's were 'Cloak and Gown Specialists'.

This beautiful shop window display was at Sugden's at 37 Drake Street. H. Sugden was described at the time of this photograph as 'Toilet Specialists', although their shop had originally been a homeopathic chemist's.

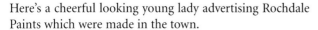

The rag and bone man used to be a familiar sight until recent years.

Here's a cheerful looking young lady advertising Rochdale Paints which were made in the town.

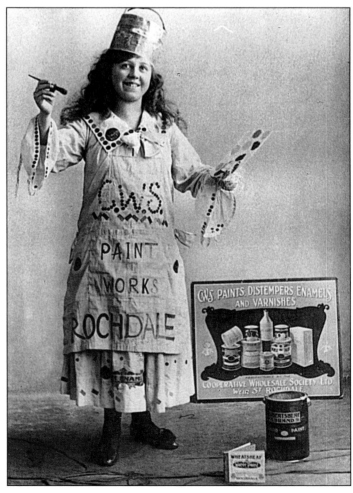

Rochdale's UCP tripe van used to be a familiar sight on the streets of the town. UCP stood for United Cattle Products.

This photograph from around 1950 shows a proud display by the Wellfield Dairy Company.

These advertisements at Manchester Road, Castleton, should bring back some nostalgic memories.

Looking up Drake Street in the early 1960s. Note the Pioneers' famous Fashion Corner and the more recently departed Iveson's on the right.

Custom Cakes Ltd on the old inside market in the early 1970s.

A market scene in 1975. Note how skirts have become shorter. Bradley's Records is on the left.

The Market Café at the old inside market at the same period.

A scene in the old indoor market just prior to demolition.

A year on and in 1976 and it's the end for the old market. Wood's, the last stall in the old Market Hall, awaits demolition.

Haworth's on South Parade was the town's number one department store – the Pioneers apart, of course.

Didn't We Have a Lovely Time?

In 1900 the Royal Lancashire Agricultural Show, then as now a great event, was held at Greenhill, Rochdale.

Richard Heape, Master of the Rochdale Hunt, outside the Egerton Arms, Ashworth, in 1900.

An idyllic Whit Friday scene in 1903 on the Vicarage Fields (now the site of Sparrow Hill School) with St Chad's in the background.

Easter is always a good time to get out into the countryside and that's what's happening here in the Ashworth Valley in 1906. A small band prepares to play in the improvised bandstand.

Building a rushcart was a skilled task. This one was built in Lower Place, Rochdale in 1906 to celebrate the Municipal Jubilee of the borough.

This splendid little paddle steamer was one of the attractions at Hollingworth Lake in the early years of the 20th century.

This was the scene at the traditional rushbearing in Whitworth around 1910.

When winters were winters and Hollingworth Lake froze over, out came the ice skaters.

Ready to show off its services in a parade around 1910, is Rochdale Steam Laundry's imaginative float, with six youngsters no doubt eager to be the centre of attraction.

The streets of Norden are lined with onlookers as Bagslate Wesleyan Chapel celebrates its centenary in 1910. The chapel, on the left, has now gone.

A Whit Friday procession at the junction of Halifax Road and Albert Royds Street around 1910.

The Millcroft Tea Gardens at Norden still serve refreshments to hungry and thirsty ramblers. But this must be a very early picture because there is no sign of the famous grove of monkey puzzle trees, nor of the swingboats which were also built here (though they no longer survive). The house bears the inscription 'Millcroft Fruit Gardens' and fruit bushes can be seen in the foreground.

Millcroft Tea Rooms are still a popular place with walkers. But it used to face competition from the Carr Wood Tea Rooms further down the Ashworth Valley. The main building still stands today, alongside the Rochdale Way, and the writing which can be seen clearly on its gable wall in the picture can still just about be deciphered.

Paddle boats became a popular attraction at Hollingworth Lake around 1920.

A football match in the 1920s.

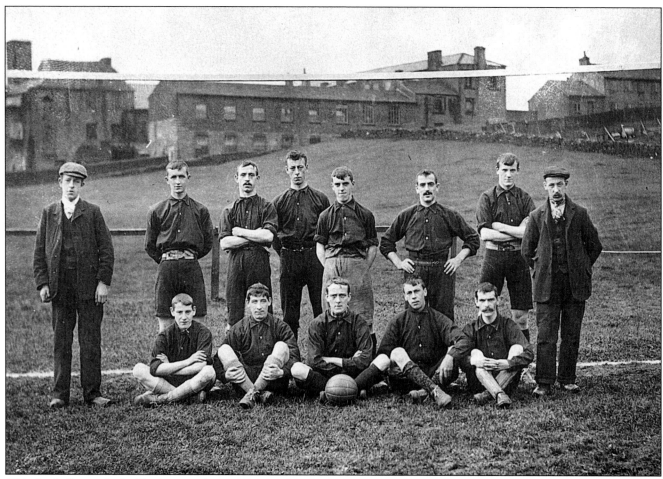

This football team looks like it meant business. Not everyone wore shorts!

A holiday postcard looks forward to the return to work when the Wakes Weeks are over with this picture of the items a weaver would take to work.

Mr W. Schofield, of Littleborough, pictured with his Knurr and Spell frame. This once popular local sport (played outdoors of course) involved hitting the porcelain knurr for as far as possible.

Fun was simpler then. Members of a local youth club enjoy a singalong around the piano at a party in 1959.

Whitsuntide processions gathered in the Town Hall Square in 1956.

Jean Bowker performs her ceremonial duties as Miss Rochdale in May 1960.

The 1960s saw a revival of many traditional events and festivities alongside the revival in folk music. Here pupils from Belfield Community School are taking part in the Pace Egg play, featuring a triumphant looking St George in this Easter-time tradition.

Hollingworth Lake has been the scene of some novel activities over the years. This picture from the 1970s shows contestants in a bath race. This was just one of several daredevil activities organised by Bill Williams and the Rochdale Adventure Club. Some baths were even turned into 'tubmarines'!

In 1974 Rochdale CHA Rambling Club celebrated its 90th anniversary with a ramble to Brown Wardle Hill above Whitworth. Pictured setting off from Market Street are Frank Butterworth, Brian Appleton, Jim Williamson, Fred Greenhalgh, Maurice Crabtree, Leaster Crossley, Norman Middleton, Dennis Holroyd, William and Phyllis Gilbody, Marian Fidler, Mary and Rachel Berry, Anthony Crossley, William Kay and Thomas Berry.

It's 1975 and the Wardle Pace Egg play comes to its dramatic end. The participants are the Wardle Methodist Players.

Rochdale Fair on The Holme showing the new college building under construction and Knowl Moor and Rooley Moor rising above the sea of chimneys. The building on the right is the old County Court.

Open Day at the English Teaching Centre, Tweedale Street, in 1978.

A sizzling scene from Littleborough Carnival in 1980.

All the fun of the fair at Rochdale Carnival in 1980 on the Town Hall square.

It's samosas and mince pies at Wardleworth Community Centre in August 1993.

Rochdale Model Boat Club held its regatta at Syke Pond in 1980. Residents recently succeeded in restoring the ponds to their former glory.

May Day celebrations at Oakenrod School in 1978 with May Queen Kulzan Nisa.

The 50th anniversary Pace Egg play at Balderstone School in March 1978.

Rochdale's Ukrainian community marching in protest against the holding of Ukrainian prisoners in the then USSR; April 1974.

Anti-racism march on Trafalgar Street, Rochdale, led by Joel Barnett MP and Councillor John Connell in 1978.

Relaxing at home – time for a quick drink after school and a spot of 'telly' before tea.

Rochdale's singing sensation Lisa Stansfield, prior to international fame and fortune, helps at Rochdale AFC's Lottery stall in 1982.

Rochdale's rushbearing was proudly revived in 1986. What price another go?

The 'Muslims' cricket team which reached the final of Rochdale Cricket League's Senior Cup in 1982.

Life in Norden and Bamford

An aerial view of Bamford in 1966 when this formerly rural area was beginning to disappear under a sea of modern housing. Just showing, at the bottom right, is part of Bury Road. Running across the top of the picture Bamford Way is under construction with Northdene Drive running down off it towards the impressive gardens at the bottom of the photograph.

Another view of Bamford taken at the same time. War Office Road runs up from the bottom of the picture to meet Norden Road. The houses of South View and Porritt's Mill are on its left and work is beginning on Wordsworth Way on the right.

Mill and housing for the workers at Red Lumb, Norden. The mill has now been converted into flats. This picture was taken about 1930.

Tenterhouse at Norden was the former home of the Hutchinson family and later used for a short time as a Roman Catholic college. After World War One it housed Belgian refugees. Later it was the site of the Riviera swimming pool (pictured in *Images of Rochdale*). Now a development of modern houses stands here.

Norden Primary School and Edenfield Road in an early aerial photograph.

Not the sort of scene we associate with up-market Norden today. But this was Back Norry Street as recently as 1968.

Life in Littleborough and Wardle

Wardle Square was always the centre for village events. Here the band plays, banners are carried proudly and the women and girls are in their Sunday best for a church walking day.

The Square is quieter on this shot with passengers preparing to board the bus around 1920. In the background can be seen the Wardle Co-operative store.

This footbridge at Wardle used to be popular with walkers. Known as 'Uncle Tommy Bridge' it took its name from Mr J.T. Howarth who owned land locally. Stewart Bank Farm is in the background.

Another view of Uncle Tommy Bridge.

The scene at Smallbridge in 1905 when the road was being dug up (nothing new there then) in preparation for new tram lines.

This picture in Littleborough around 1910 shows two of Rochdale's tram fleet.

An outing from Gale House at Littleborough, the home of the Scott family.

A well-groomed horse and anxious lady outside Stubley New Hall.

Wardle agricultural fair in 1907 with St James's Church on the right.

A scene from the Soldiers and Sailors Carnival at Wardle in September 1917, which raised money to provide comforts for the troops. The man with the donkey was known as 'Little Crick'.

A quiet scene in the centre of Wardle village in 1976.

Wardle Fold around 1910.

Trap Lane, Wardle, in the early years of the 20th century.

Looking along Wardle Road.

A parade along Ramsden Road, Wardle in 1890.

A newer side of Wardle. Armstrong Hurst Close in 1980.

Summit from Temple Lane, Littleborough around the end of the 19th century. This was a raw, hard-working landscape in those days.

This scene from Lydgate in 1981 shows the famous 'Hanging Gate' which once publicised the Lydgate Inn. The name 'Lydgate' means postern gate. The inn, which dated from the late 18th century was one of the oldest in the Rochdale area. It was originally called the 'Lydiet'. In the 20th century it had somewhat a chequered career and from 1942 until 1975 it was a private house. After this it became both a pub and a night club which achieved notoriety in the 1980s for its topless bargirls. Less controversially it was used to film part of the TV series *Travelling Man*. In June 1987, the building burnt down.

A view of Littleborough in 1987, taken from Windy Bank on the Blackstone Edge Old Road. Law's mill is on the left.

Whittaker hamlet above Hollingworth Lake is still a picturesque spot today. The wood is now in the care of the Woodland Trust. Running through the middle of it can just be made out the old watercourse into which water was pumped from Hollingworth Lake to be taken to the head of the canal at Summit.

The Last of the Giant Pig

Mr. John Alletson's big pig has been so much talked about in the village that the following account of its last end will be read with interest. It is taken from the Blackpool Herald, "Mr. Robinson, pork butcher, did a grand stroke of business when he secured the 'infant' or perhaps to be more accurate we should say 'The Empress,' a pretty little pig which was fed by Mr. John Alletson, of Littleborough, and which when alive weighed 54 score, and when slaughtered drew the scale at 43 score 7 lbs. Considering that the animal was only 27 months old it may be credited with having made the best use of its time. We confess we never saw such a pig before. It was well proportioned, and in all respect a splendid animal. That it attracted attention will be easily understood when we say that between five and six thousand persons passed through Mr. Robinson's shop on Wednesday evening. The crush was something enormous." We are informed that the weight of the leaf lard taken from the animal was 50 lbs., pulling lard 25 lbs., one ham 98 lbs., the head 63 lbs., and the two kidneys $1\frac{1}{3}$ lbs.

Life in Milnrow and Newhey

Going down into Newhey on the Denshaw Road. The spire of St Thomas's Church can just be seen in the distance. This area, close to the junction of the lane to Ogden, is known as Flannel Brow. The terraced houses were obviously new when this was taken. Look at how clean they are, in spite of the smoke that drifts across the picture.

The *Observer*'s bill was to the fore outside William Stock's newsagent's shop in Dale Street, Milnrow in 1905.

These youngsters with the donkey in a back alley at Milnrow were half-timers. Their time was split between schooling and work at the mill.

Wildhouse Lane at Milnrow is well known. Here is the building that gave it its name, pictured in 1907.

The opening of Milnrow Library in 1907.

A proud display of carts at John Fielding's coal merchants at Newhey.

Staff and vehicles of Newhey coal merchants John Fielding and Son Ltd lined up proudly to be photographed. This family firm was founded in the 1890s and the Fieldings did much for Milnrow and Newhey. Abraham Fielding presented Milnrow UDC with its chairman's chain of office. The two pictures were presumably taken some years apart.

Milnrow Fire Brigade on Harbour Lane on Whit Friday 1924.

A peaceful scene of handloom weavers' cottages at Lane Bottom, Newhey.

Clogs and shawl were still in evidence when this picture was taken at Huddersfield Road, Newhey, in 1920.

This very early picture shows the Wildhouse area of Milnrow, an area now submerged by housing.

One of the best known names in early Milnrow was the Stump and Pie Lad pub, allegedly named after a one-legged fell runner.

Dale Street, Milnrow, in 1979.

Life Up Healey and Whitworth Way

Two pictures of Millgate at Shawforth; the earliest taken in 1914 and the latest around 1960 show how much this area changed in the intervening years. A common theme is the hills and the sweep of the railway line. The dominating mill and its chimney have disappeared and the rows of houses in the centre of the picture have lost their chimney stacks. The later picture shows new homes being built along the line of the old rail track.

A single-decker tram and covered wagon on Market Street, Whitworth, around 1910.

A view of life from the past at Healey Hall. This was the home of the Heape family, most notably the huntsman Richard Heape. Heape was a man of many parts and among his many passions was one of collecting date stones; particularly those from buildings which were being demolished or had fallen into disrepair. The house and grounds today contain dozens of these; a real history book of the district.

The outside of Healey Hall when its gardens were in their prime.

This towering rushcart was a feature of the Whitworth Parish Church Carnival of 1910.

Looking south along Healey Bottoms in 1933. Today the Healey Dell Visitor Centre is in part of the mill complex at the centre of the picture.

Healey Bottoms looking up towards the viaduct in 1906.

Steam comes up from a train at Station Road, Facit.

This proud little steam engine hauled stone from Britannia Quarry at Facit.

Hard Times and Disasters

The funeral of Thomas Pickles, chief engineer at John Bright and Brothers Fieldhouse Mill, brought crowds on to Whitworth Road. He died in a boiler house accident in 1906.

The grave of Mr Pickles at Rochdale Cemetery was bedecked with flowers.

One lad excepted, there doesn't seem to have been much to smile about in Littleborough in 1912 when people were queuing for tickets to get coke during the coal strike.

Digging for Victory at Newhey School during World War One. That's rather a splendid cabbage!

Tents for recuperating servicemen in the grounds of Birch Hill Hospital in 1916.

This card was produced to promote Rochdale Tank Week in April 1918 when funds were being raised to help purchase what at the time were the very latest war technology.

Gracie Fields visits the Salvation Army soup kitchen in the Depression.

Sandbags at the ready outside Rochdale Post Office during World War Two.

Evacuees, on Rochdale Station in World War Two, waiting for the train to Bacup.

American aid for Rochdale's war effort in the dark days of 1941. Dr Morgan MP hands over a thousand-dollar cheque to the Mayor, Alderman E.H. Scarr. This was almost a year before the US officially joined the conflict.

This dramatic picture shows bomb damage at Holborn Street, Sudden, in 1941. This was the scene of the town's only fatality of the January bombing raid.

More bomb damage from the same raid. This time the scene is Manchester Road.

This was the damage caused by a bomb at Belfield.

The Civil Defence parades outside the Cenotaph in 1941.

On 27 March 1949, the nine-year-old son of an auxiliary fireman lost his life when he became buried in this sand pit at Sudden. Rescuers failed to get him out alive.

An action scene from 1953 with PCs Ogden and 'Sailor' Gooderham and their dog Kim.

A Rochdale emergency. These pictures from the 1950s show the aftermath of a nasty accident between a lorry and a motorbike. The first shows the scene looking up John Street towards Whitworth and the second looks along Yorkshire Street towards Heybrook.

A dramatic scene as lighting strikes over Meadway in 1960.

St James's Church, Ashworth, after the disastrous fire in 1960.

Re-opening the road over Blackstone Edge was a big task during the famous winter of 1963.

Snow could even be a problem at lower levels. Traffic queuing along Oldham Road in January, 1963.

The dramatic scene in July 1972 when a demolition contractor working on the Entwisle Road viaduct accidentally triggered off this spectacular collapse on Halifax Road. Luckily no one was hurt, but the incident drew crowds of onlookers as well as more official visitors.

This was the dramatic and never-to-be-forgotten scene in 1974 when the Summit railway tunnel caught fire. Smoke and flames can be seen rising high into the air from one of the tunnel vents.

Going to Blazes

Fires in old cotton mills could be sudden and spectacular. Oils given off by the processing of the cotton over the years made surfaces coated with them highly inflammable. In cases where cotton was not the culprit other, equally inflammable materials, were usually to blame. This and the great height of many of the mills meant tackling a blaze could be a real challenge for the local fire brigade. Some spectacular blazes over the years included:

* Nov. 1923 Dixon's Soap Works on Canal Street.
* Jan. 1926 Sladen Mill, Littleborough.
* Aug. 1930 Ormerod's Leather Works.
* Dec. 1937 Rochdale Market Hall.
* Nov. 1939 A & W Law's Durn Mill.
* Oct. 1949 Davey Kenyon's mill on Mellor Street.
* Jun. 1952 Clover Mill.
* Nov. 1954 Theatre Royal
* Nov. 1956 Peel Mill, Shawforth.
* Sep. 1958 Fletcher Bolton's sawmill.
* Feb. 1960 Dunlop Mill.
* Feb. 1961 Rochdale Motor Panel and Engineering Ltd, Hudson Street Works.
* Apr. 1961 Dexine Rubber Co, Norden.
* March, 1969 College of Art, Fleece Street.

Fire at Robinson's in July 1922.

These next four pictures show dramatic scenes from the blaze which destroyed Sparth Mill in May 1975. This former cotton mill was home at the time to the Lancashire Wallpaper Supply Company, a big wallpaper and paint distributor.

These shots of Dunlop Mill in February 1960 shows the immense damage caused by a spectacular fire there. Worse still, a brave and long-serving employee who was trying to tackle the flames with a hosepipe, was killed when the ceiling collapsed on him. It had always been the management's proud boast that the buildings were fireproof, but the fire occurred in a part of the building which had recently been taken over by Dunlopillo which involved the storing of foam rubber. Fire engines from all over Lancashire, joined by others from Cheshire and Yorkshire, fought desperately to control the blaze. But, when this was at last achieved, millions of pounds of damage had been done. By a stroke of great irony it was National Fire Prevention Week!

Getting About a Bit

Built to carry stones from quarries in Bacup and Whitworth to Rochdale, the Rochdale to Bacup rail line has to cross Healey Dell. In order to do this the magnificent Healey Dell Viaduct had to be built (pictured under construction in 1867). The River Spodden had to be diverted while this happened.

The building of a new bridge over the canal at Firgrove in 1906. The steam engine in the background looks a splendid workhorse.

Rochdale's last horse-drawn bus outside the Liberal Club in Norden. The terminus for the service was at the Brown Cow.

The motor bus was king now. Here we see the pulling up of the tramlines and relaying of the setts on the Butts. You can see what a painstaking task the latter was. They would have looked (and worn) better than the modern version we have today.

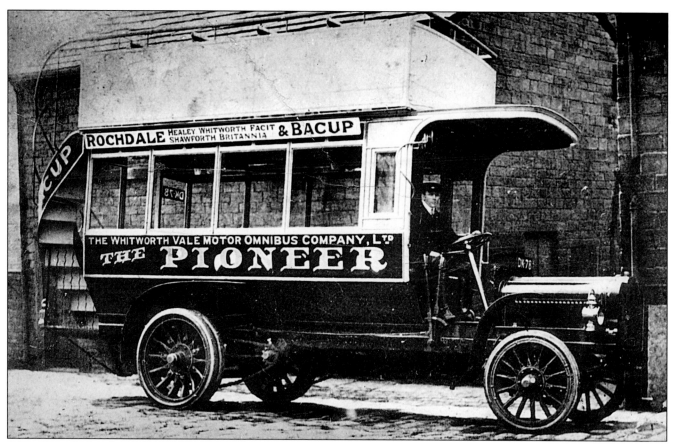

From 1906 to 1909 this early motorbus connected Whitworth with the outside world.

A study in buses. Looking east over Rochdale centre was a completely different prospect to that offered today. The mill of Kelsall and Kemp still dominates with more mills behind.

This smart looking vehicle, ideal for excursions, was run by Albert Holden Laws, licensee of the Tanners Arms, in the early 1930s.

Waiting for trams in Rochdale town centre in 1925.

Opposite page: Did tramway laying cause problems for the Wardleworth Cycle works?

ELECTROPLATING
WORKS.
ROAD
CRUETS
SPOONS

A. WHITELEY
WARDLEWORTH CYLE WORKS
CYCLES
PEDERSEN
PEDERSEN
PEDERSEN

A weighty steam traction engine officially tests Hamer Lane bridge for strength in 1925.

A study in buses.
Rochdale town centre in
1960.

A rare aerial view of Healey Dell in times past. Notice the train going over the viaduct and the fact that there are far fewer trees than nowadays. Healey Hall is at the top right of the picture.

An aerial view of the Littleborough to Rochdale canal, rail line and road in 1966.

You needed a head for heights if you were one of the workmen building the Rakewood Viaduct in 1966-67. The bridge, more than 100ft above the valley running down into Hollingworth Lake, carries the M62 up on to the Pennines.

The widening of Molesworth Street bridge in 1979 must have caused considerable traffic chaos.

What About the Workers?

It's haymaking time at Brown Wardle Farm on the slopes above Watergrove.

Cutting the hay using 'one-horse power' on the shores of Hollingworth Lake.

Hard at work building electricity meters at the Rochdale Electric Co. Ltd around 1900.

Youngsters carrying coke from the Rochdale gasworks during the coal strike in 1912.

The Rochdale Electric works.

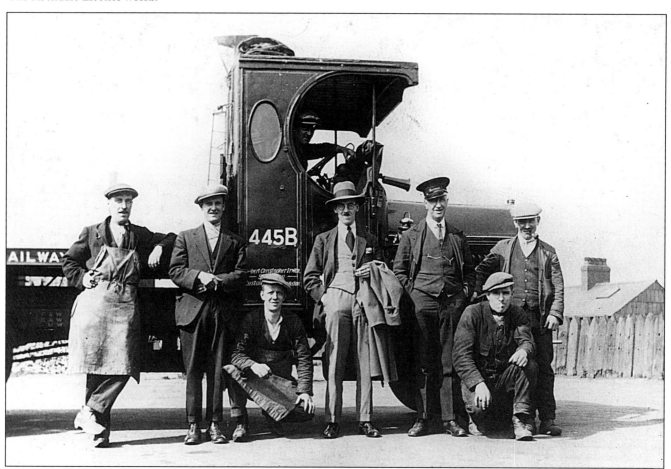

Workers at the railway goods yard.

Healthy Minds & Healthy Bodies

It is sad but true that litter has always been a problem in Rochdale in spite of the numerous exhortations to clean up. This was the message in the Trades Procession of 1928, which was a big day in the life of the town.

This cart had been making a similar appeal in the Trades Procession the year before.

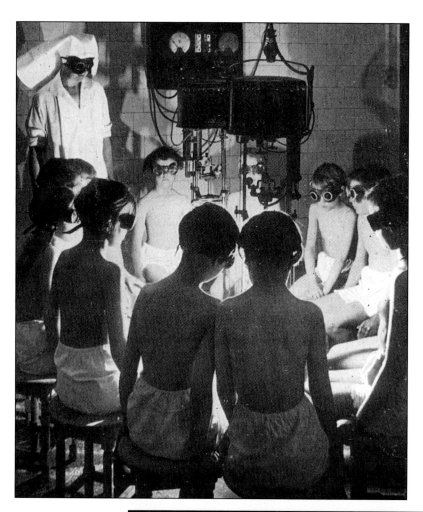

Fresh air and sunshine (which does increase the body's production of Vitamin D, the lack of which causes rickets) were deemed good for children from Rochdale's back streets. There was an open air school at Brownhill. An alternative was artificial sunlight treatment at Rochdale Infirmary which in 1928 treated 23,153 patients.

This Cleansing Department poster from World War Two shows there's nothing new about recycling.

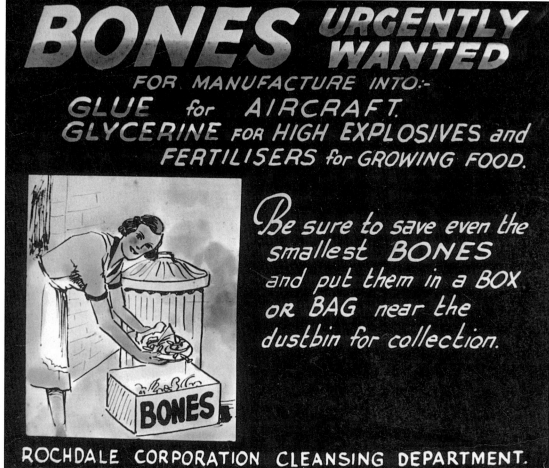

BONES URGENTLY WANTED
FOR MANUFACTURE INTO:-
GLUE for AIRCRAFT.
GLYCERINE FOR HIGH EXPLOSIVES and
FERTILISERS for GROWING FOOD.

Be sure to save even the smallest BONES and put them in a BOX or BAG near the dustbin for collection.

BONES

ROCHDALE CORPORATION CLEANSING DEPARTMENT.

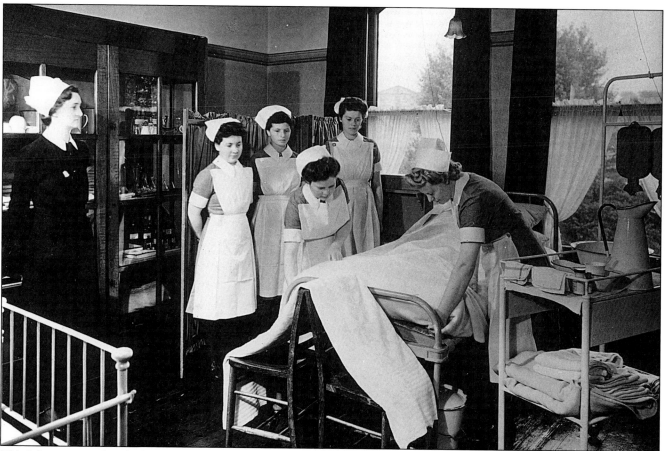

This is how you make a bed! Young nurses in training at Rochdale Infirmary around 1960.

Building Smallbridge branch library in 1971.

A youngster gets assistance in the Junior Department of Rochdale Central Library in 1975.

This picture of Sparrow Hill School from 1980 brings home how much Rochdale has changed in its buildings and social make-up over the years. But children's playground activities stay much more constant.

Praise the Lord!

An old painting of Bamford Congregational Chapel in 1861 shows the school, chapel and manse that are familiar today. On the left, though, is the original Sunday school, now gone, where Dr Kay (later Sir James Kay-Shuttleworth) was superintendent and where he formulated his ideas for day school education, which were to lead to the setting up of England's school system. Dr Kay's cousins, John and James Fenton of Bamford Hall, also taught here on Sundays.

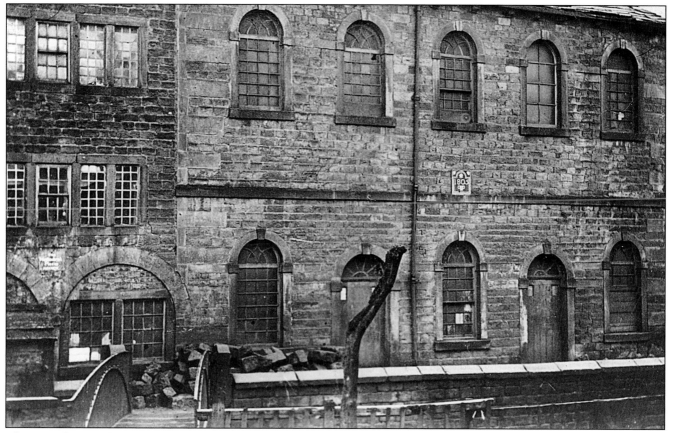

The quaintly named Methodical Piazza stood at Bridge End, Littleborough, near the railway. Note the 1805 datestone.

A drawing of the Hope Chapel and School in Rochdale. The chapel still stands to this day.

Smithy Nook Chapel (Mount Gilead) around 1910. This church which belonged to the Methodist New Connection was built in 1817.

St John's Church and the Fire Station brought a new style of architecture to Maclure Road. St John's was built in the Byzantine style on the plan of the famous cathedral of St Sophia in Istanbul. The dome is 68ft in diameter. The church was opened, in June 1925, by the Archbishop of Westminster. The Fire Station, which opened in 1935, cost what seems a bargain £29,000 to build on the site given by Alderman Robert Turner a few years before; yet another example of what Rochdale owes to the family asbestos firm. The most spectacular feature of the building was the 115ft tower for drying hose pipes. Alongside it were built 32 new houses for the firemen.

The Firm That Built Rochdale

One name above all is associated with innumerable Rochdale buildings – that of Howarth. As far back as 1750 there was a building firm of this name with Samuel Howarth as its head. The business was continued by Simon's son and grandson. The latter had two sons, Robert and Thomas, who worked separately but joined forces after the death of their father to form R. & T. Howarth in 1900. In the decades to come their firm built many cotton mills and public buildings; so much so that the town we see undoubtedly owes more to them than anyone else. What follows are some examples of their work undertaken by 1900 and 1940.

Robert and Thomas Howarth.

Messrs Tweedale and Smalley's Works, built at Castleton in 1901, was one of the town's leading engineering works.

State Mill, on Moss Bridge Road, Rochdale, the first cotton mill built by the firm in 1900. By the 1930s it had amalgamated with the nearby Croft and Clover Mills; the joint company becoming one of the largest cotton spinners in the area.

Arrow Mill on Queensway later became part of the giant Courtauld's group, specialising in man-made fibres.

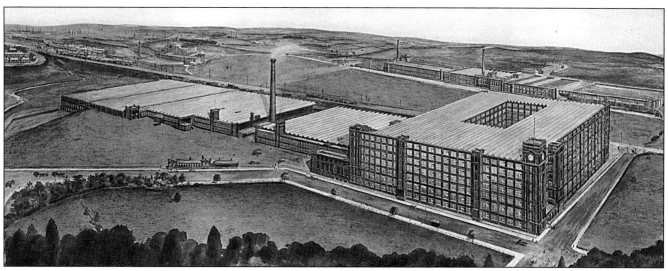

Dunlop Cotton Mills at Castleton.

Turf Hill housing estate was part of the enormous house-building programme which Rochdale Council undertook between the wars and which also included the Spotland and Kirkholt estates.

The Farewell Inn, Castleton, stands on the site of an earlier pub used as a recruiting base during the Napoleonic Wars. Young men were persuaded (having been bought more beer than was good for their long-term well being) to sign up for King and Country. The result was the tearful farewells that gave the pub its name.

The Golden Ball Hotel on Spotland Road, Rochdale, was built in 1911, but retained stained glass depicting an eagle from an earlier pub on the site.

The Richard Bentley Smalley Memorial Hall at Castleton.

The *Rochdale Observer* printing works on School Lane in 1925. The building later became the editorial and administrative offices.

The Rialto Cinema, Rochdale, was opened on 27 August 1928 by Rochdale's superstar Gracie Fields.

The Yorkshire Penny Bank.

The Post Office on the Esplanade was planned as early as 1911, but due to World War One and its aftermath was not opened until 1927. The architect of this fine building, thankfully recently restored to its original function, was designed by the Post Office's in-house architect C.P. Wilkinson.

The Thomas Champness Memorial Hall on Drake Street.

Rochdale Baths on Entwisle Road.

Electric House was the home of the town's electricity company.

The billiards room, ballroom and conservatory at the Rhyddings, Castleton.

The Kingsway Hotel.

The 1930s Rochdale Market Hall under construction.

Relining the reservoir at Birch Hill.

Bridging over the Roch.